1st Edition August 2022

If you find an error in this book, please email **support@quovadimusmedia.co.uk** *with a description of the error and the page number.*

About Quo Vadimus Media Ltd

We are a learning & media company based in the United Kingdom, using evidence-informed practice to help individuals and businesses to learn and improve in a changing world. We bring a wealth of knowledge from schools, colleges, universities, and academic research to improve learning.

Our services and products are based on and developed from over 25 years of experience in the self-improvement and education sectors.

We provide online learning as well as producing print & digital publications to enhance learning and retention of knowledge.

Website: **https://quovadimusmedia.co.uk**

About the Author

Graeme Lamb is the founding Director of Quo Vadimus Media Ltd, a lecturer in accountancy at a college of Further Education in the northwest of England, and a practising bookkeeper holding AATQB (qualified bookkeeper) status with the AAT.

About this Book

This book is a pocket revision guide for those studying the AAT level 2 unit, Introduction to Bookkeeping. It is not intended to be a complete course of study.

Financial and Management Accounting

There are two main types of accounting.

Financial Accounting	Management Accounting
Financial accounting involves preparing materials for an external audience (e.g., HMRC, shareholders).	Management accounting involves preparing materials for an internal audience (e.g., managers, directors).
Based on the financial activity of the business, recording transactions, and preparing financial statements.	Based on current trends, looking forward to the future (e.g., costing and budgeting).
Is often based on international accounting standards and local legislation and must be produced to agreed standards (e.g., financial statements).	Is often based on international accounting standards but has more flexibility in how information is presented to internal audiences (e.g., monthly budget reports).

Bookkeeping

What is Bookkeeping?

Bookkeeping is about keeping the financial records of the business, in either a paper-based or computerised form. The practice of bookkeeping is governed by principles and practices that have developed over hundreds of years, as well as international standards and legislation.

A range of different approaches exist to bookkeeping, but throughout the world, the most common system used is **double-entry bookkeeping**.

Bookkeeping also involves using the bookkeeping records to prepare end-of-year financial statements and accounts. Bookkeeping is part of what is known as **financial accounting**.

Making Tax Digital & VAT

Maxing Tax Digital will require businesses to make their financial submissions to HMRC for **VAT** (Value Added Tax) and other matters using compatible digital software rather than paper-based returns and submissions, with very few exceptions.

What is VAT?
VAT, more properly known as **Value Added Tax**, is an indirect tax on consumption that is charged on most goods and services. Businesses that are VAT-registered are required to charge VAT on goods and services that they sell according to the rules set down in the relevant government legislation. They must also provide a timely return to HMRC, resulting in either money paid to or money reclaimed from HMRC.

VAT Calculations
Many of the calculations in this unit will involve sums that are either inclusive or exclusive of VAT, the latter sometimes being referred to as net of VAT. **Including VAT** = VAT at 20% has already been included. *Example: £120.00 including VAT (£100 net + £20 VAT) To determine how much VAT has been added to a VAT-inclusive figure, divide by 6, e.g., £120 / 6 = £20. This is also known as the VAT fraction.* **Excluding VAT** = VAT at 20% has NOT already been included. *Example £100.00 excluding VAT (£100 net but £20 VAT has not yet been added) To determine how much VAT to add to a net figure, divide by 5, e.g., £100 / 5 = £20.*

Computerised Accounting

Modern, computerised accounting systems have various advantages over paper-based systems, including:

- Import transactions from numerous different sources, including bank records, CSV files (comma-separated values, often from spreadsheet programs), and other third-party software.
- The ability to automatically total and balance accounts.
- Automatically post from daybooks and other books of prime entry to the General Ledger.
- Automatically reconcile Receivables/Payables Ledgers to the relevant control accounts.
- Automatically generate a trial balance or audit trail.
- Process recurring entries.

However, disadvantages of these systems also can occur, created by:

- Misunderstanding of how the software works, or how data should be entered or imported.
- Errors in original documents.
- Errors in data entry by bookkeepers and accountants.

Information that is incorrectly entered, whether in a manual or digital bookkeeping system, can cause a cost to the business, both financially and in terms of reputation or lost business.

Types of Sale or Purchase

Cash Sale	A sale that the business has made where payment has been made immediately.
Cash Purchase	A purchase that the business has made where payment has been made immediately.
Credit Sale	A sale where payment is made at a later date, according to payment terms set by the seller.
Credit Purchase	A purchase where payment is made at a later date, according to payment terms set by the seller.

Cash and credit sales and purchases may, or may not, be paid in cash. The terms cash and credit give no indication as to the method of payment, only the time of payment.

Transaction Locations

Financial transactions will be recorded in a number of different locations, depending on the type and nature of the transaction.

Books of Prime Entry	The first place in the accounting system where a financial transaction is recorded.
Day books	Books of prime entry for recording transactions around credit sales and credit purchases only.
Double-entry	The main bookkeeping of the accounting system for many businesses, recorded in individual accounts in what are known as ledgers, as described below.
Receivables Ledger	A collection of individual accounts (credit customers) to which the business has sold on credit.
Payables Ledger	A collection of individual accounts (credit suppliers) from which the business has bought on credit.
General Ledger	A collection of individual accounts for a variety of different types of transactions within the business, covering a range of transactions. Often numerically arranged in categories.

Account Categories

Accounts in the General Ledger can be placed into various different categories. Dividing transactions and accounts in this way allows for an easier understanding of what a particular account, or transaction, means for the business.

Capital	Money put into the business by the owner(s).
Drawings	Money taken out of the business by the owner(s).
Assets	Money owed by credit customers to the business, or items of value owned by the business, or the value of money held.
Liabilities	Money owed to credit suppliers by the business, or the value of money owed by the business to other parties.
Income	Money received by the business from selling goods or services, or other sundry income.
Expenses	Money spent by the business as part of its general running costs.
Purchases	Money spent by the business on raw materials or finished goods with the intention of selling them to customers.

Double-Entry Bookkeeping

Double-entry bookkeeping is so-called for the following reasons:

- Each transaction is usually* recorded as a pair of entries.
- One entry will be in one account, whereas the second entry will be in another account.
- The two accounts involved will be determined by the nature of/reason for the transaction.
- One account will contain the debit entry, one account will contain the credit entry.
- The two sides must match, the debit entry must equal the credit entry.

In some cases, there will be three entries rather than two. This is often the case when there are transactions involving VAT.

Accounts in the General Ledger, as well as those in the Receivables or Payables Ledger, are set out in what is known as a 'T' account format, with the **left-hand side for debit entries** and the **right-hand side for credit entries**. It is commonly the case the debit entry is entered before the credit entry, a convention that will often be followed in this book.

Bank Account (1200)	
Debit *(dr)* £	Credit *(cr)* £

Rule 1 — Bank and Cash Accounts

This first rule applies when dealing with bank payments/receipts or cash payments/receipts, and only applies to accounts that can be considered as bank accounts.

Money In =	Money Out =
Debit	Credit

Money being paid into the bank would be recorded on the **debit** side of the Bank Account, and money being paid out of the bank would be recorded on the **credit** side of the Bank Account. This rule would also apply equally to the Cash Book, or Cash Account or the Petty Cash Book or Petty Cash Account, or any account involving money transactions, e.g., a Bank Deposit Account. It would not apply to a Bank Loan Account, which would be considered as a liability account.

An example of this is where capital (money introduced to the business by the owner) has been paid into the account. This example will be looked at more closely later, with only the debit entry shown here. This is money coming into the business, and so is recorded as a debit in the Bank Account. The date format here (01-01) refers to the day and the month, January 1st.

Bank Account (1200)		
Debit *(dr)* £	Credit *(cr)* £	
01-01 Capital 20,000		

Rule 2 – DEAD CLIC

For all other accounts in the General, Receivables or Payables Ledger, DEAD CLIC, DEAP CLIC, or PEARLS are sometimes used.

There is some controversy over the extent to which these ways of learning double-entry are helpful. They are generally helpful at level 2 when learning the principles of double-entry. However, in the long term, it is more helpful to have a deep understanding of how different types of accounts behave, rather than just memorising methods such as these.

DEAD CLIC

Debits	Credits
Expenses will normally have a debit balance but may have some transactions on the credit side.	Liabilities will normally have a credit balance but may have some transactions on the debit side.
Assets will normally have a debit balance but may have some transactions on the credit side.	Income will normally have a credit balance but may have some transactions on the debit side.
Drawings will normally have a debit balance but may have some transactions on the credit side.	Capital will normally have a credit balance but may have some transactions on the debit side.

DEAP CLIC

Debits	Credits
Expenses will normally have a debit balance but may have some transactions on the credit side.	Liabilities will normally have a credit balance but may have some transactions on the debit side.
Assets will normally have a debit balance but may have some transactions on the credit side.	Income will normally have a credit balance but may have some transactions on the debit side.
Purchases will normally have a debit balance but may have some transactions on the credit side.	Capital will normally have a credit balance but may have some transactions on the debit side.

PEARLS

Purchases will normally have a debit balance, but may have some transactions on the credit side
Expenses will normally have a debit balance, but may have some transactions on the credit side
Assets will normally have a debit balance, but may have some transactions on the credit side
Revenue will normally have a credit balance, but may have some transactions on the debit side
Liabilities will normally have a credit balance, but may have some transactions on the debit side
Sales will normally have a credit balance.

Assets & Liabilities

Current & Non-Current Assets & Liabilities
Current assets and liabilities are usually short-term, often meaning less than a year. Examples include bank and cash balances, money owed by credit customers or to credit suppliers. Non-current assets and liabilities are usually longer term, often over a year. Examples include loans and mortgages.

Assets
Assets are an item that is owned by the business and has a reasonable amount of value, or money owed to the business by a customer who has bought goods on credit. It could also be: • The balance of the Bank Account if there is money in the bank. • The balance of the VAT Account if money is owed by HMRC (a debit balance). • Any cash held by the business (for example, petty cash, or the balance of the Cash column in the Cash Book). It is usually relatively straightforward to decide whether something a business owns should be viewed as an asset, as it is usually something that has value and could be used, if necessary, to meet debts and other commitments.

Liabilities

A liability is an amount of money that the business owes to a third party. This could be a loan or an amount owed to a supplier after buying goods on credit.

It could also be:

- The balance of the Bank Account if it is overdrawn.
- The balance of the VAT Account if VAT is owed to HMRC.
- The balance of a credit card that has not yet been paid.
- Wages yet to be paid to employees, or other payroll-related liabilities (pension fund or trades union contributions, income tax/National Insurance owed to HMRC).

The Accounting Equation

There are various means by which an accountant or bookkeeper can use information from the accounts of the business to either gauge the health of the business or to draw conclusions about the business.

If it is desirable to calculate the amount of capital within the business, one method is the **accounting equation**. The accounting equation calculates the amount of capital in the business by comparing it to the amount of assets and liabilities.

The formula is:

Assets — Liabilities = Capital

This formula is also the basis of the **Statement of Financial Position** that many businesses are required to produce each year as part of their required financial statements.

The other formula generally required by businesses is the **Statement of Profit or Loss**. The formula is:

Income — Expenses = Profit
(or loss if the answer is a negative figure)

The Statement of Profit or Loss shows the income and expenses of a business over a 12-month period, to determine whether the business is making a profit or loss.

Balancing Accounts

Balancing a bookkeeping account manually has various steps:
1. Add up each side of the account (debit and credit).
2. Create a transaction on the smaller side numerically (this is called the balance carried down).
3. Total both sides, which should now be the same amount.
4. Create a transaction on the side which was larger numerically (this is called the balance brought down).

Each of these steps can be seen in turn:

Step 1: Add up each side of the account

Bank Account (1200)				
Debit *(dr)*		**Credit *(cr)***		
£		£		
01-01 Capital	20,000	01-01 Machinery	15,000	
01-01 Bank Loan	25,000	01-01 Raw Materials	13,500	

The sum of the debit side is £45,000, the sum of the credit side £28,500.
The difference between the two sides (£45,000 - £28,500 = £16,500) must then be entered into the Bank Account:

Step 2: Enter the balance carried down

Bank Account (1200)				
Debit *(dr)*		**Credit *(cr)***		
£		£		
01-01 Capital	20,000	01-01 Machinery	15,000	
01-01 Bank Loan	25,000	01-01 Raw Materials	13,500	
		01-01 Balance c/d	**16,500**	

The balance carried down (abbreviated as the balance c/d) is always dated on the last date of the period in question, in this case, January 1st, or it could be the last day of the week of the month, as appropriate.

The two sides of the account are then calculated again, and they should be identical.

Step 3: Add the new totals for both sides of the account

Bank Account (1200)				
Debit *(dr)* £		**Credit** *(cr)* £		
01-01 Capital	20,000	01-01 Machinery	15,000	
01-01 Bank Loan	25,000	01-01 Raw Materials	13,500	
		01-01 Balance c/d	16,500	
Total	**45,000**	Total	**45,000**	

It is worth noting that the totals will always be the sum of the higher side, in this case, £45,000, and that the balance c/d is the transaction that makes the two sides balance, hence balancing the account.

The balance c/d, however, is not the true balance of the account, because it is on the wrong side, as that is added in the final step.

Step 4: Add the balance brought down

Bank Account (1200)				
Debit *(dr)* £		**Credit** *(cr)* £		
01-01 Capital	20,000	01-01 Machinery	15,000	
01-01 Bank Loan	25,000	01-01 Raw Materials	13,500	
		01-01 Balance c/d	16,500	
Total	**45,000**	Total	**45,000**	
02-01 Balance b/d	**16,500**			

The fact that the balance is brought down on the debit side indicates that the account has a debit balance. As the Bank Account records the balance as an asset (if the business has money) or a liability (if the business is overdrawn), this means that a debit balance in the account indicates that the business has £16,500 in the bank.

Credit Purchases

The key sales & purchases documents are:

Document Types	
Price Quotation	A document provided by the seller of goods and services, outlining the price the buyer will pay should they place an order.
Purchase Order	A document provided by the buyer of goods and services, outlining to the seller the goods and services they wish to buy.
Invoice	The key document provided by the seller, outlining the items sold, the cost of those items, and when/how the buyer should pay.
Goods Received Note	A document completed by the buyer, which acknowledges receipt of the goods purchased.
Credit Note	A document provided by the seller to the buyer when goods or services are returned or are incomplete and reduces the value of the invoice to which it relates.
Statement of Account	A document sent by the seller to the buyer outlining the balance of the account and any related transactions.

Price Quotation

A document provided by the seller of goods and services, outlining the price the buyer will pay should they place an order.

Price Quotation	
From:	**To:**
FabFrames Ltd 25 Meadowcroft Estate Ashwell AS19 2HF VAT No: 145853235	Delta Q Bikes Ltd Unit 3b Ashwell Business Park Ashwell AS17 4BX VAT No: 798204391
Item(s) & Price: 10 x Electric Blue bicycle frame, £90.00 excluding VAT.	
Signed: *C Chambers*	**Date:** 28/12/2021

Price quotations may or may not include VAT.

Purchase Order

A document provided by the buyer of goods and services, outlining to the seller the goods and services that they wish to buy.

Purchase Order

From:	To:
Delta Q Bikes Ltd Unit 3b Ashwell Business Park Ashwell AS17 4BX VAT No: 798204391	FabFrames Ltd 25 Meadowcroft Estate Ashwell AS19 2HF VAT No: 145853235
Purchase Order No: PO452	**Date:** 30/12/2021

Product Code	Quantity	Description
EBFM	10	Electric Blue bicycle frame

Authorised:	Date:
G Kenworthy	30/12/2021

Purchase orders may include price information and VAT if this is the case.

A purchase order will not usually be accepted by the seller if there is no signature indicating official authorisation by the buyer.

Invoice

> The key document provided by the seller, outlining the items sold, the cost of those items, and when/how the buyer should pay.

Invoice

From:	To:
FabFrames Ltd 25 Meadowcroft Estate Ashwell AS19 2HF VAT No: 145853235	Delta Q Bikes Ltd Unit 3b Ashwell Business Park Ashwell AS17 4BX VAT No: 798204391

Invoice no:		Account		Your reference:		Date:	
FF431		DEL001		PO452		01/01/2022	

Product Code	Description	Quantity	Price £	Unit	Total £	Discount %	Net £
EBFM	Electric Blue Frame	10	90.00	each	900.00	0.00	900.00

Terms: 60 days		Goods Total	£900.00
Carriage paid		VAT	£180.00
E&OE		Total	£1080.00

An invoice is the most common document exchanged between buyer and seller. It must include details about the buyer and seller, VAT of the seller (if registered, information about the product, pricing, and calculations.

It will also include the coding for the purchase order that led to the invoice, if one was given.

Goods Received Note

A document completed by the buyer, which acknowledges receipt of the goods purchased. This may be provided by the seller or the buyer.

Goods Received

From:		To:	
FabFrames Ltd 25 Meadowcroft Estate Ashwell AS19 2HF VAT No: 145853235		Delta Q Bikes Ltd Unit 3b Ashwell Business Park Ashwell AS17 4BX VAT No: 798204391	
Goods received note no:	**Your reference**	**Date:**	
FFGR198	PO452	02/01/2022	
Product Code	**Quantity**	**Description**	
EBFM	10	Electric Blue Frame	
Received by:		**Date:**	
S Kenworthy One bike frame damaged		02/01/2022	

A Goods Received Note may be completed by the buyer on receipt of the goods to acknowledge the quality and quantity of goods received as correct or incorrect. This Goods Received note acknowledges that one bike frame is damaged.

The template may be provided by either the seller or the buyer.

Credit Note

> A document provided by the seller to the buyer when goods or services are returned or are incomplete and reduces the value of the invoice to which it relates.

Credit Note

From:	To:
FabFrames Ltd	Delta Q Bikes Ltd
25 Meadowcroft Estate	Unit 3b
Ashwell	Ashwell Business Park
AS19 2HF	Ashwell
	AS17 4BX
VAT No: 145853235	VAT No: 798204391

Credit note no: CRN215		Reason for credit: 1 frame damaged	

Invoice no:	Account	Your reference:	Date:
FF431	DEL001	PO452	03/01/2022

Product Code	Description	Quantity	Price	Unit	Total	Discount %	Net
EBFM	Electric blue frame	1	90.00	each	90.00	0.00	90.00
					Goods Total	90.00	
					VAT	18.00	
					Total	108.00	

A credit note looks very similar to an invoice, and is often linked to a particular invoice, as in this case. Credit notes can be issued for other reasons, such as discounts, as shall be seen later. Although in a real transaction, FabFrames Ltd may have sent a bicycle frame to replace the one that was damaged, the credit note process for a return here is shown as part of the learning process.

Statement of Account

> A document sent by the seller to the buyer outlining the balance of the account, and any related transactions.

Statement of Account

From:	To:
FabFrames Ltd 25 Meadowcroft Estate Ashwell AS19 2HF VAT No: 145853235	Delta Q Bikes Ltd Unit 3b Ashwell Business Park Ashwell AS17 4BX VAT No: 798204391

Account: DEL001	Date: 31/01/2022

Date	Details	Debit £	Credit £	Balance £
01/01/2022	Balance b/f			0.00
01/01/2022	Invoice FF431	1080.00		1080.00
04/01/2022	Credit note CRN215		108.00	972.00

Payments may be made electronically to FabFrames Ltd Sort code: 01-26-91 Account no: 45813290	Total:	£972.00

A statement of account should list all transactions for the time period and provide a suggestion as to means of payment. Statements of account may be issued according to the wants of the supplier, e.g., weekly or monthly, and can also be issued on demand. In modern accounting, many businesses are often able to log in to an online account and see their balance with a supplier at any time.

Discounts Received

Discounts can be offered by a supplier (seller) to a customer (buyer) for one of three reasons:

Discount Types	
Trade Discount	Usually offered to regular customers as a set percentage, as an incentive to keep buying from that supplier.
Bulk Discount	Usually offered when purchases are over a certain level (either in percentage, unit or monetary terms).
Prompt Payment Discount *(PPD)*	An incentive offered to encourage customers to pay earlier than the agreed invoice terms.

Calculated on the invoice and forming part of the invoice total:
- Trade Discount
- Bulk Discount

These amounts are discounted from the net amount on the invoice and must be discounted from the net before VAT is added.

Mentioned on the invoice but only calculated if the customer pays within the agreed time limit:
- Prompt Payment Discount

This amount is not calculated on the invoice but will be calculated from the total (gross) amount when the customer pays, presuming that they have met the conditions of the PPD as mentioned in the invoice.

Invoice (with trade or bulk discount)

This invoice shows a discount of 10%, which is discounted from the net, prior to VAT and the gross total being calculated. Both trade and bulk discounts behave in this manner.

Invoice

From:				To:			
FabFrames Ltd 25 Meadowcroft Estate Ashwell AS19 2HF VAT No: 145853235				Delta Q Bikes Ltd Unit 3b Ashwell Business Park Ashwell AS17 4BX VAT No: 798204391			

Invoice no:		Account		Your reference:		Date:	
FF431		DEL001		PO452		01/01/2022	

Product Code	Description	Quantity	Price £	Unit	Total £	Discount %	Net £
EBFM	Electric Blue Frame	10	90.00	each	900.00	10.00	810.00

Terms: 60 days					Goods Total	£810.00
Carriage paid					VAT	£162.00
E&OE					Total	£972.00

Trade discount is offered to beneficial customers in order to encourage them to buy. Different percentages may be offered to different customers.

Bulk discount is offered to customers who buy over a certain amount. Bulk discount is often, but not always, offered at the same % to all customers.

Invoice (with prompt payment discount)

This invoice shows a prompt payment discount of 5%, which is not calculated on the invoice.
If Delta Q Bikes Ltd pay the invoice within 7 days, they will:

a) Pay 95% of the gross total of the invoice (invoice amount minus 5% PPD).

b) Receive a credit note subsequently from FabStyle for the value of the discount - £54.00 (£45.00 net, £9.00 VAT). Both businesses will enter the credit note into their relevant accounting systems, and the invoice will show as paid.

Invoice

From:				To:			
FabFrames Ltd 25 Meadowcroft Estate Ashwell AS19 2HF VAT No: 145853235				Delta Q Bikes Ltd Unit 3b Ashwell Business Park Ashwell AS17 4BX VAT No: 798204391			

Invoice no:		Account		Your reference:		Date:	
FF431		DEL001		PO452		01/01/2022	

Product Code	Description	Quantity	Price £	Unit	Total £	Discount %	Net £
EBFM	Electric Blue Frame	10	90.00	each	900.00	0.00	900.00

Terms: 60 days			
Carriage paid	Goods Total	£900.00
E&OE	VAT	£180.00
PPD - 5% if paid within 7 days of invoice	Total	£1080.00

Coding

Businesses are free to use any coding system they prefer for customer codes, invoicing, purchase orders, credit notes etc. Sometimes, businesses will inherit codes from the system suggested by their computerised accounting software, although businesses are free to change those codes as best suits their needs.

Coding can be:

Numeric – just numbers, e.g., 123

Alphabetic – just letters, e.g., ABC

Alphanumeric – a combination of numbers and letters, e.g., ABC123

The latter is the most common.

Common coding systems are:

POXXX – purchase orders, where PO stands for purchase order, XXX is a number to indicate which purchase order, e.g., PO123.

INVXXX – invoices, where INV stands for invoice, XXX is a number to indicate which invoice, e.g., INV001.

CNXXX – credit notes, where CN stands for credit notes, XXX is a number to indicate which credit note, e.g., CN456.

Another common coding system you will see in your studies is customer and supplier coding, e.g.

HAR001 – this is a common code for a company called Harper Limited.

HAR002 – this could be used for another company with a similar name, e.g., Harper PLC.

You should be aware that in some computerised accounting systems, once a code has been assigned to a customer or supplier, it may not be possible to change it.

As well as using codes for documents, customers and suppliers, businesses will also use General Ledger codes to analyse purchases. The most common code range used in the General Ledgers for purchases is in the 5000-5999 range.

Credit & Cash Purchases

Credit purchases = buy now, pay later. An invoice is sent with the goods, and the buyer pays within the prescribed payment period.

Cash purchases = buy now, pay now. The payment takes place at the same time as the transfer of ownership of the goods.

The term credit or cash refers to the nature of the transaction (buy now pay later or buy now pay now), not the payment method. The terms cash and credit can have multiple meanings in accountancy and bookkeeping. When transferring transactions involving VAT from purchases-related day books to ledgers, it is always the case that:

- There will be two credits and one debit, or two debits and one credit.
- The sum of the credits will equal the sum of the debits.
- One account will always be the Payables Ledger Control Account.
- One account will always be the VAT Account.
- The other account will be named after the relevant day book.

Purchases

Purchases Day Book						
Date	Details	Invoice	PL Code	Net £	VAT £	Total £
01-01	FabFrames Ltd	FF431	FAB001	900.00	180.00	1080.00
08-01	WonderWheels	PIN276	WON001	750.00	150.00	900.00
10-01	SuperSuspension	INV561	SUP001	235.00	47.00	282.00
			TOTALS:	1885.00	377.00	262.00

Total	This is transferred to the **Payables Ledger Control Account**. This sum records the **liability** that is owed to suppliers and is a credit.
VAT	This is transferred to the **VAT Account**. This sum records the reduction of the **asset** that is owed from HMRC and is a debit, as it can be reclaimed from HMRC.
Net	This is transferred to the **Purchases Account**. This sum records the expected expenses from purchases and is a debit.

As well as being recorded in the General Ledger, the purchases will also be recorded in the supplier accounts in the Payables Ledger. The behaviour of the Payables Ledger and Payables Ledger Control Account are identical, as both accounts record the value of the liability (the purchase) still owed to the supplier.

Purchases Returns

Purchases Returns Day Book						
Date	Details	Credit note	PL Code	Net £	VAT £	Total £
03-01	FabFrames Ltd	CRN215	FAB001	90.00	18.00	108.00
15-01	WonderWheels	PINC276	WON001	10.00	2.00	12.00
16-01	SuperSuspension	INVC561	SUP001	4.00	0.80	4.80
			TOTALS:	104.00	20.80	124.80

Total	This is transferred to the **Payables Ledger Control Account**. This sum records the **reduction of the liability** that is owed to suppliers and is a debit.
VAT	This is transferred to the **VAT Account**. This sum records the **reduction of the expense** that can be claimed from HMRC and is a credit, as it cannot be reclaimed.
Net	This is transferred to the **Purchases Returns Account**. This sum records the **reduction of the expense** from purchases and is a credit.

As well as being recorded in the General Ledger, the purchases will also be recorded in the supplier accounts in the Payables Ledger. The behaviour of the Payables Ledger and Payables Ledger Control Account are identical, as both accounts record the value of the liability (the purchase) still owed to the supplier. The details PRDB are used to explain where the information came from.

Discounts Received

Discounts Received Day Book						
Date	Details	Credit note no:	PL Code	Net £	VAT £	Total £
05-01	FabFrames Ltd	CRN218	FAB001	40.50	8.10	48.60
			TOTALS:	40.50	8.10	48.60

This discount received amount represents 5% of £972.00. The original invoice total from FabFrames Ltd was £1080.00. This was reduced by the credit note by £108.00 due to a damaged frame, making the final total due £972.00. The original invoice indicated a PPD (prompt payment discount) if it was paid within 7 days. The invoice was sent on January 1st and paid on January 5th so therefore a discount was appropriate.

Total	This is transferred to the **Payables Ledger Control Account**. This sum records the **reduction of the liability** that is owed to suppliers and is a debit.
VAT	This is transferred to the **VAT Account**. This sum records the **reduction of the expense** that can be claimed from HMRC and is a credit.
Net	This is transferred to the **Discounts Received Account**. This sum records the **amount of the reduction given by suppliers as an income** (expense reduction) and is a credit.

As well as being recorded in the General Ledger, the discounts received will also be recorded in the supplier accounts in the Payables Ledger. The behaviour of the Payables Ledger and Payables Ledger Control Account are identical, as both accounts record the value of the liability (the purchase) still owed to the supplier.

Payables Ledger Control Account

Payables Ledger Control Account (2100)					
Debit £					Credit £
31-01	PRDB	124.80	30-11	PDB	2,262.00
31-01	DRDB	48.60			
31-01	Bank	923.40			

The Payables Ledger Control Account is a liability account. Liability accounts have credit balances.

Credit entries:

- A credit purchase, which creates a liability.

An entry on the credit side of the Payables Ledger Control Account is only used to increase the amount owed to the supplier.

Debit entries:

- A purchase return, which reduces a liability
- A discount received, which reduces a liability
- A payment, which reduces a liability

An entry on the debit side of the Payables Ledger Control Account is only used to decrease the amount owed to the supplier.

Remittance Advice

This is a document often sent by a customer to a supplier to indicate what they have paid and to what items/invoices/credit notes it relates.

Remittance Advice			
From: Delta Q Bikes Ltd Unit 3b Ashwell Business Park Ashwell AS17 4BX		**To:** FabFrames Ltd 25 Meadowcroft Estate Ashwell AS19 2HF	
Date: 05/01/2022			
A payment of £923.40 was made by bank transfer on 05/01/2022, relating to the following invoice and adjustments.			
Date	**Our Ref**	**Your Ref**	**Amount £**
01/01/22	PO452	FF431	1080.00
03/01/22	PO452	CRN215	(108.00)
05/01/22	PO452	FF431 (PPD @ 5%)	(48.60)

Computerised accounting packages are capable of producing a remittance advice as a document, which can then be printed to send to a supplier or sent via email.

A remittance advice is often sent:
1. As an attachment to an email to indicate that an electronic payment has been made, or
2. As a printed document sent along with a cheque to indicate the reason for the cheque.

More informally, a remittance advice may simply take the form of the accounts person at one company informing another accounts person at another company by email or phone that a payment has or is about to be made.

Analysed Purchases Day Book

A business that chooses to analyse its purchases at a deeper level within the bookkeeping may use an analysed day book. An analysed day book replaces the single net column (which would normally be the purchases account) with relevant columns for different purchase types.

	Purchases Day Book						
Date	Details	Invoice	PL Code	Purchases - Bikes	Purchases – E-bikes	VAT £	Total £
			TOTALS:				

In an analysed day book, the VAT and Total columns would be recorded as normal, but the relevant purchases (net) would be used to signify the different categories of purchase, with each given a separate General Ledger code – for example, 5000, 5001.

It is common for businesses that make multiple product types to analyse purchases in this way, as it provides better storytelling regarding the cost of purchases for different parts of the business.

General Ledger for Purchases

Purchase		
	Debit	**Credit**
Purchases	✓	
VAT	✓	
Payables Ledger Control Account		✓
Purchase Return		
	Debit	**Credit**
Payables Ledger Control Account	✓	
Purchases Returns		✓
VAT		✓
Discount Received		
	Debit	**Credit**
Payables Ledger Control Account	✓	
Discounts Received		✓
VAT		✓
Payment of Invoice		
	Debit	Credit
Payables Ledger Control Account	✓	
Bank		✓

Credit and Cash Sales

Credit sales = buy now, pay later. An invoice is sent with the goods and the buyer pays within the prescribed payment period.

Cash sales = buy now, pay now. The payment takes place at the same time as the transfer of ownership of the goods.

The term credit or cash refers to the nature of the transaction (buy now pay later or buy now pay now), not the payment method. The terms cash and credit can have multiple meanings in accountancy and bookkeeping. When transferring transactions from sales-related day books to ledgers, it is always the case that:

- There will be two credits and one debit, or two debits and one credit.
- The sum of the credits will equal the sum of the debits.
- One account will always be the Receivables Ledger Control Account.
- One account will always be the VAT Account.

The other account will be named after the relevant day book.

Sales

Sales Day Book						
Date	Details	Invoice	RL Code	Net £	VAT £	Total £
02-02	Northlynch Bikes	DQB001	NOR001	1500.00	300.00	1800.00
04-02	Westernpool Cycles	DQB002	WES001	625.00	125.00	750.00
			TOTALS:	2125.00	425.00	2550.00

Total	This is transferred to the **Receivables Ledger Control Account**. This sum records the **asset** that is owed by customers and is a debit.
VAT	This is transferred to the **VAT Account**. This sum records the **liability** that is owed to HMRC and is a credit.
Net	This is transferred to the **Sales Account**. This sum records the expected **income** from sales and is a credit.

As well as being recorded in the General Ledger, the sales will also be recorded in the customer accounts in the Receivables Ledger. The behaviour of the Receivables Ledger and Receivables Ledger Control Account are identical, as both accounts record the value of the asset (the sale) still owed by the customer.

Sales Returns

Sales Returns Day Book						
Date	Details	Credit note	PL Code	Net £	VAT £	Total £
07-02	Westernpool Cycles	CN001	WES001	110.00	22.00	132.00
			TOTALS:	110.00	22.00	132.00

Total	This is transferred to the **Receivables Ledger Control Account**. This sum records the **reduction of the asset** that is owed to suppliers and is a credit.
VAT	This is transferred to the **VAT Account**. This sum records the **reduction of the liability** that is owed to HMRC and is a debit.
Net	This is transferred to the **Sales Returns Account**. This sum records the **reduction of the income** from purchases and is a debit.

As well as being recorded in the General Ledger, the sales will also be recorded in the customer accounts in the Receivables Ledger. The behaviour of the Receivables Ledger and Receivables Ledger Control Account are identical, as both accounts record the value of the asset (the sale) still owed by the customer. The details SRDB are used to explain where the information came from.

Discounts Allowed

Discounts Allowed Day Book						
Date	Details	Credit note no:	SL Code	Net £	VAT £	Total £
08-02	Northlynch Bikes	CN002	NOR001	37.50	7.50	45.00
			TOTALS:	37.50	7.50	45.00

Total	This is transferred to the **Receivables Ledger Control Account**. This sum records the *reduction of the asset* that is owed by customers and is a credit.
VAT	This is transferred to the **VAT Account**. This sum records the *reduction of the liability* that is owed to HMRC and is a debit.
Net	This is transferred to the **Discounts Allowed Account**. This sum records the **amount of the reduction given to customers as an expense** (income reduction) and is a debit.

As well as being recorded in the General Ledger, the discounts allowed will also be recorded in the customer accounts in the Receivables Ledger. The behaviour of the Receivables Ledger and Receivables Ledger Control Account are identical, as both accounts record the value of the asset *(the sale)* still owed by the customer.

Analysed Sales Day Book

A business that chooses to analyse its sales at a deeper level within the bookkeeping may use an analysed day book. An analysed day book replaces the single net column (which would normally be the sales account) with relevant columns for different purchase types.

	Sales Day Book						
Date	Details	Invoice	PL Code	Sales - Bikes	Sales - E-bikes	VAT £	Total £
			TOTALS:				

In an analysed day book, the VAT and Total columns would be recorded as normal, but the relevant purchases (net) would be used to signify the different category of sale, with each given a separate General Ledger code – for example, 4000, 4001.
It is common for businesses that make multiple product types to analyse in this way, as it provides better storytelling regarding the sales income for different parts of the business.

General Ledger for Sales

Sales		
	Debit	**Credit**
Sales		✓
VAT		✓
Receivables Ledger Control Account	✓	
Sales Return		
	Debit	**Credit**
Receivables Ledger Control Account		✓
Sales Returns	✓	
VAT	✓	
Discount Allowed		
	Debit	**Credit**
Receivables Ledger Control Account		✓
Discounts Allowed	✓	
VAT	✓	
Payment of Invoice Received		
	Debit	Credit
Receivables Ledger Control Account		✓
Bank	✓	

Receivables Ledger Control Account

Receivables Ledger Control Account (2110)				
Debit £				Credit £
31-01	SDB	2550.00	08-02 Bank	1755.00
			28-02 SRDB	132.00
			28-02 DADB	45.00

The Receivables Ledger Control Account is an asset account. Asset accounts have debit balances.

Debit entries:

- A credit ale, which creates an asset.

An entry on the credit side of the Payables Ledger Control Account is only used to increase the amount owed to the supplier.

Debit entries:

- A sales return, which reduces an asset
- A discount allowed, which reduces an asset
- A payment received, which reduces an asset

An entry on the debit side of the Receivables Ledger Control Account is only used to decrease the amount owed by the customer.

The Cash Book

The Cash Book is the book of prime entry and the double-entry bookkeeping for most transactions involving income and expenditure in the business.

In many modern computerised accounting systems, there may not be a Cash Book, but rather there will be a Cash Account and a Bank Account in the General Ledger. However, some accounting software still allows specifically for a Cash Book.

In a larger business or financial department, there may be a Cashier who has the prime responsibility for the Cash Book.
In a manual accounting system, the Cash Book is typically laid out in the following manner:

Cash Book							
Date	Details	Cash	Bank	Date	Details	Cash	Bank

As with other double-entry accounts, there is a debit and a credit side, with space for multiple transactions on each side.

What is different with the Cash Book is that rather than just one place for entering the amount on each side, there are separate columns for cash and bank.

Cash specifically refers to notes and coins.

Analysed Cash Book

It is common to use an analysed Cash Book, which means that as well as columns for Cash and Bank (which are double-entry), a business can be free to use other columns as suits the business best. These analysed columns are prime entry rather than double-entry and require a further entry in the General Ledger in the relevant account, on the opposite side to their entry in the Cash Book.

Cash Book — Debit £							
Date	Details	Cash	Bank	Trade Receivables	VAT	Cash Sales	Other Income
01-03	Balance b/d		17,331.60				
02-03	Westernpool Cycles		618.00	618.00			
08-03	Online sales		1,530.00		255.00	1,275.00	
15-03	Online sales		1,179.60		196.60	983.00	
16-03	Bank Interest Received		1.50				1.50
18-03	Contra	500.00					
			TOTALS:	618.00	451.60	2,258.00	1.50

Cash Book — Credit £							
Date	Details	Cash	Bank	Trade Payables	VAT	Cash purchases	Other Expenses
05-03	Super Suspension		888.00	888.00			
05-03	WonderWheels		277.20	277.20			
11-03	Wages		3,160.00				3,160.00
13-03	Insurance		1,200.00				1,200.00
13-03	Rent		3,000.00				3,000.00
15-03	Bank Charges		10.00				10.00
18-03	Drawings		2,500.00				
18-03	Contra		500.00				
19-03	Petty Cash	200.00					
			TOTALS:	1,165.20			7,370.00

The analysed totals need to be added up once all transactions are entered, and the Cash and Bank columns balanced separately. Cash can only be brought down on the debit side, the Bank column can be brought down on either side according to the balance.

A contra entry indicates money taken out of the Bank column and placed in the Cash column, or vice versa.

Recurring Items

A business may have several transactions that can be identified as **recurring items**, known in some accounting software as **recurring entries**.

Recurring items are usually items that are regular payments, although depending on the business, they can also be receipts.

Examples could include:
- Rent
- Insurance
- Bank Loan (although no payments have yet been made on the bank loan)

Recurring items are usually those payments (or receipts) that stay static for some time, so a year's worth of insurance with 12 identical monthly payments on the same date, or a year's rent with 12 identical monthly payments on the same date, are ideal candidates.

Utility bills such as water, electricity or gas are also suitable candidates if they are a regular fixed direct debit or standing order (students will study these payment methods more in the next unit). Variable utility bills would not be appropriate as recurring items.

Most accounting software has a facility for adding recurring items. It is usually a case of setting up the relevant payment from the bank in the software, and then setting it up as a recurring item. This will normally involve setting up the date (for example, 13th of the month) and the frequency (for example, monthly) of the transaction. This automation of recurring items can help minimise the amount of work required to enter certain transactions, as well as budgeting and reporting for expected upcoming costs using the bookkeeping records of the business.

The Petty Cash Book

The Petty Cash Book behaves in a very similar manner to the Cash Book, in that it is both a book of prime entry and double-entry, in this case for small cash (notes and coins) transactions only.

There are three main differences between the Petty Cash Book and the Cash Book:

- It only deals with cash (notes and coins), so there is no need for Cash and Bank columns. There is instead a single Amount column.
- It deals mostly with payments, although receipts are possible, particularly when it is being topped up.
- It often has a system for topping up at regular intervals.

Petty Cash Book							
Date	Details	Amount	Date	Details	Amount	VAT	Stationery	Other Expenses
				Totals:				

The Imprest System

Many businesses that use a Petty Cash Book or a similar system will follow what is known as the imprest system.

In an imprest system, the petty cash is topped to a set amount at the beginning of every time period, e.g., weekly or monthly, as appropriate.

Imprest System
A business starts the month with £100.00 in its Petty Cash Book.
During the month, the business spends £75.50, leaving it with a balance of £24.50.
At the end of the month, ready for the beginning of the next month, £75.50 is withdrawn from cash (in the Cash Book) and transferred into the Petty Cash Book, to restore the balance of £100.00.
The same procedure is followed at the end/beginning of every month.
This is an imprest system.

In this case, the double-entry to restore the imprest would be:

Account	Debit £	Credit £
Petty Cash	75.50	
Cash		75.50

Petty Cash Voucher

Many businesses will use petty cash vouchers as part of the authorisation process. Most employees will not just be able to spend petty cash as and when they wish, as the business will most likely have policies regarding how money is spent and who may spend it.

For each of the expenses, a petty cash voucher is created.

The petty cash voucher is an important part of the authorisation process. A petty cash voucher may look like this:

Petty Cash Voucher	Voucher no: 098
	Date: 20/03/2022
Details:	Amount £:
Tea	12.00
Coffee	9.00
VAT	4.20
Total:	25.20
Signed:	*C Cheshire*
Authorised	*TL Bentley*

Balancing the Petty Cash Book

A Petty Cash Book with an Imprest System should restore the imprest, then balance the account as usual.

Petty Cash Book								
Date	Details	Amount £	Date	Details	Amount	VAT	Stationery	Other Expenses
19-03	Cash	200.00	20-03	Office Expenses	25.20	4.20		21.00
23-03	Stamps	5.00	21-03	Stationery	51.00	8.50	42.50	
31-03	Cash	133.70	23-03	Stamps	15.00			15.00
			25-03	Train Travel	47.50			47.50
			31-03	Balance c/d	200.00			
		338.70			338.70			
01-04	Balance b/d	200.00						
				Totals:		12.70	42.50	83.50

When using the Imprest System, the balance carried down and the balance brought down are the same amount that the account is restored to at the beginning of the next period, £200.00. With a Petty Cash Book that uses the imprest system, this will always be the case, as long as the imprest is (correctly) restored before the account is balanced.

A common error that students make when restoring imprest is to, rather than restoring the imprest from the amount of expenses (plus any income), attempt to restore the imprest amount as the balance of the account, rather than the amount spent.

Petty Cash Reconciliation

When balancing the Petty Cash Book, it is important to check that the balance of the Petty Cash Book matches the amount of petty cash that is actually held by the business. This process is called **reconciliation**.

Ensuring that this process is as smooth as possible, and that the amount of cash held is correct can be ensured by following procedures, such as:

- Petty cash being kept in a locked and secure tin.
- Limited authorisation of access to petty cash.
- Regular balancing and reconciliation.
- Reimbursement of petty cash amounts spent, rather than giving money out ahead of the expenditure.
- Use of petty cash vouchers to confirm authorisation of expenditure.
- Insistence of receipts and other documentation for all petty cash purchases.

Petty Cash Book	Date: 08/08/2021
£50 notes	£0.00
£20 notes	£20.00
£10 notes	£20.00
£5 notes	£5.00
£2 coin	£4.00
£1 coin	£11.00
50p coin	£2.50
20p coin	£0.80
10p coin	£0.90
5p coin	£0.55
2p coin	£0.14
1p coin	£0.01
Balance of Petty Cash in hand £	64.90
Balance of Petty Cash Book £	64.90

Printed in Great Britain
by Amazon

31201789R00030